F L O U R I S H

Finding your place for wholeness and fulfillment

STUDY GUIDE

For foreign and subsidiary rights, contact the author.

Cover design: Eric Powell
Cover photo: Andrew van Tilborgh

ISBN: 978-1-957369-21-1   1 2 3 4 5 6 7 8 9 10

Printed in the United States of America

F L O U R I S H

Finding your place for wholeness and fulfillment

MICHAEL TURNER

AVAIL

CONTENTS

INTRODUCTION

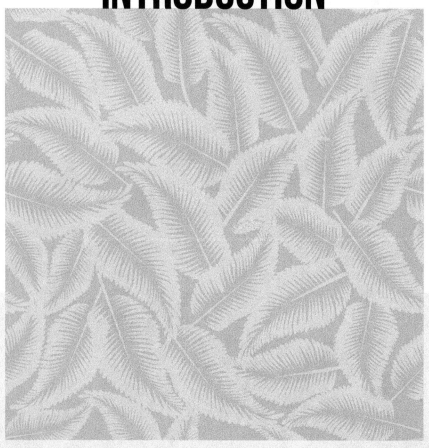

"The house of God (the local church) is not a building; it is
the dwelling place of God, where we can connect with His
presence and His people, so we can fulfill His purpose."

As you read the Introduction in *Flourish*, review, reflect on, and respond to the text by answering the following questions.

REVIEW, REFLECT, AND RESPOND:

What do you hope to gain from this study (for example, a better understanding of the purpose behind the local church, a closer sense of intimacy with God and/or His people, etc.)?

_____

_____

_____

_____

_____

_____

_____

_____

_____

_____

Do you find it difficult to connect with the local church? Why or why not?

_____

_____

_____

_____

_____

_____

_____

_____

_____

_____

_____

_____

> "The righteous will flourish like a palm tree, they will grow like a cedar of Lebanon, planted in the house of the LORD, they will flourish in the courts of our God."
>
> —Psalm 92:12-13 (NIV)

Consider the scripture above and answer the following questions:

Why is it essential for our flourishing that we are planted in the house of God?

_____

_____

_____

_____

What other places might we "plant" ourselves in hopes of finding purpose, peace, and community?

_____

_____

_____

_____

What are the pros of these other places? How do they fall short of replacing God's body of believers?

_____

_____

_____

_____

_____

_____

_____

_____

_____

_____

_____

_____

Write a prayer asking the Lord to guide your mind and heart as you embark on this study. Lay before Him any reservations, hurts, or struggles you might have in connection with the idea of being planted in a local church. Ask for His truth, wisdom, and love to lead you as you delve into the material in these pages. Remember, the church was His idea! He is the only one who can teach us how to flourish in the church!

_____

_____

_____

_____

_____

_____

_____

_____

_____

_____

_____

_____

_____

_____

_____

MADE FOR MORE

*"The greatest gift we can give to others
is a healthy version of ourselves."*

As you read Chapter 1: "Made for More" in *Flourish*, review, reflect on, and respond to the text by answering the following questions.

REVIEW, REFLECT, AND RESPOND:

Why do you think our thoughts have such a profound influence on the way we live our lives?

_____

_____

_____

_____

_____

_____

_____

What thought patterns are currently informing or influencing your lifestyle? Are there positive trends you notice in your thoughts? What about less-than-positive trends? What unhealthy tendencies can you identify?

_____

_____

_____

_____

_____

_____

_____

_____

_____

_____

_____

How do you think about yourself? If you were asked to describe yourself to someone else, what thoughts or words come to mind first?

_____

_____

_____

_____

_____

_____

_____

Who has left a legacy in your life? Who has poured into you and shaped you?

_____

_____

_____

_____

_____

_____

Whom has God placed in your life for you to pour into, to mentor? For whom can you leave a legacy?

_____

_____

_____

_____

_____

_____

What are some concrete next steps you can take to begin moving towards living for the future and not just for the temporary things of today?

_____

_____

_____

_____

_____

_____

_____

_____

_____

> *"For the world offers only a craving for physical pleasure, a craving for everything we see, and pride in our achievements and possessions. These are not from the Father, but are from the world."*
>
> —*1 John 2:16 (NLT)*

Consider the scripture above and answer the following questions:

The world is constantly fighting to shape our thoughts, actions, and beliefs. How can involvement in/being planted in the local church begin to replace some of the world's philosophies and priorities with biblical ones?

_____

_____

_____

_____

_____

_____

In this chapter, we explored the concept of a legacy and why it's so important. How do the cravings of the world keep us from focusing on eternal things, such as leaving a legacy for those that follow?

_____

_____

_____

_____

_____

_____

_____

HOLY GROUND

"Even when the enemy of our souls tries to strip our dignity, just as he did with Adam and Eve, we can have confidence that God's house and His family have been fully restored."

As you read
Chapter 2:
"Holy Ground"
in *Flourish*,
review, reflect
on, and respond
to the text by
answering
the following
questions.

REVIEW, REFLECT, AND RESPOND:

What "houses" have you gravitated towards in your life thus far? What communities or centers have you sought to find a home in?

_____

_____

_____

_____

_____

_____

_____

What methods of the enemy to destroy God's house stand out to you? Which of the strategies written about in this chapter have you witnessed or experienced firsthand?

_____

_____

_____

_____

_____

_____

_____

_____

_____

_____

In your own words, why do you think it's so important for Satan to dismantle the house of God and cripple the people of God?

_____

_____

_____

_____

_____

God chose the church as the only place where God's presence, people, and purpose all occur at the same time! What are some of the privileges and joys that we forfeit when we don't get plugged into a local church?

_____

_____

_____

_____

_____

Generally speaking, do you find yourself glad to go to the house of the Lord during this season of your life? It's okay if you answered "no" or "not yet." What experiences, influences, and memories do you think inform your answer?

_____

_____

_____

_____

_____

_____

> *When he came to his senses, he said, "How many of my father's hired servants have food to spare, and here I am starving to death! I will set out and go back to my father and say to him: 'Father, I have sinned against heaven and against you. I am no longer worthy to be called your son; make me like one of your hired servants.'" So he got up and went to his father. But while he was still a long way off, his father saw him and was filled with compassion for him; he ran to his son, threw his arms around him and kissed him.*
>
> —Luke 15:17-20 (NIV)

Consider the scripture above and answer the following questions:

Why was it important for the prodigal son to come to this realization on his own, rather than being coerced or forced into it by his older brother or his father?

_____

_____

_____

_____

What things from home besides physical food do you think the son was missing? What hadn't he been able to find in his wild, runaway life that he craved now?

_____

_____

_____

_____

_____

_____

_____

THERE'S NO PLACE LIKE HOME

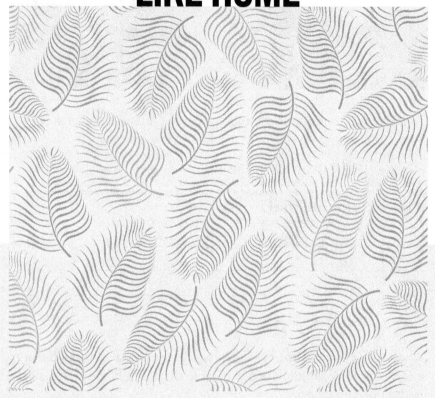

"We, as God's children, will never be orphans because we have a Father who will never give up on us and is always fighting for us."

As you read Chapter 3: "There's No Place Like Home" in *Flourish*, review, reflect on, and respond to the text by answering the following questions.

REVIEW, REFLECT, AND RESPOND:

How does it make you feel to know that God is always fighting for, interceding on behalf of, and actively loving His children?

_____

_____

_____

_____

_____

_____

In what ways were you raised to believe that your salvation and intimacy with God depended on your works?

_____

_____

_____

_____

_____

_____

Why is it essential to recognize that we can't earn God's love in our own strength?

_____

_____

_____

_____

_____

_____

Whether you grew up with a present, loving father or not, the impact of a father on his children is immense. How did your upbringing inform your perspective of God the Father?

_____

_____

_____

_____

_____

_____

_____

How can the assurance of the Father's love for us ease our struggles with insecurity?

_____

_____

_____

_____

_____

_____

Why is it essential to know God as your Father in order to be truly planted in His house? In other words, why would it be difficult to be planted in a local church without knowing God as your Father through Jesus Christ?

_____

_____

_____

_____

_____

_____

_____

How might God be calling you back into relationship with Himself and His people or into an even closer relationship? Take some time to pray and journal your thoughts.

_____

_____

_____

_____

_____

_____

_____

_____

_____

_____

_____

_____

_____

_____

> *"He who dwells in the secret place of the Most High,*
> *shall abide under the shadow of the Almighty."*
>
> *—Psalm 91:1 (NKJV)*

Consider the scripture above and answer the following questions:

How do the definitions of the words "abide" and "dwell" in this chapter expand your understanding of this verse?

_____

_____

_____

_____

_____

_____

_____

Do you think the church as a whole does a good job of encouraging believers to adhere to this "abiding" lifestyle, or has the church emphasized something else in its place?

_____

_____

_____

_____

_____

_____

_____

What kinds of growth do we see when we choose to abide in Him? What fruit can you identify in your own life?

_____

_____

_____

_____

_____

_____

_____

_____

_____

_____

_____

CHAPTER 4

HE WANTS TO STAY (HABITATION)

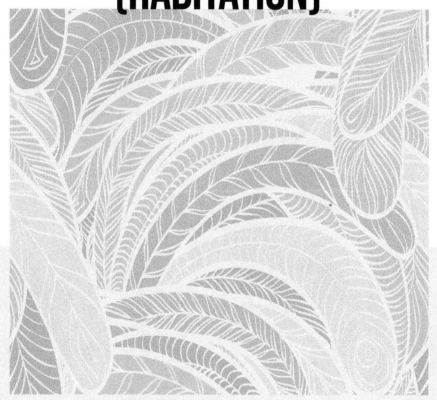

"We don't have to pray for open heavens; we just have to get under the spout and drink what's already being poured out."

REVIEW, REFLECT, AND RESPOND:

Why do you think so many churches are still praying for God to "pour out His Spirit"? How does this prayer shortchange what God has already done and keep us from fully drinking of His goodness and presence?

_____

_____

_____

_____

_____

_____

In your own words, what's the difference between a "visitation" and a "habitation"? How does shifting to a "habitation" mindset change your walk with the Lord?

_____

_____

_____

_____

_____

_____

_____

_____

_____

_____

Do you find yourself hungry for the habitation of God in His house? Again, it's okay if the answer for you right now is "no." What factors do you think play into your response?

_____

_____

_____

_____

_____

Why is humility essential to worship? How can familiarity make it challenging for us to stay humble and grateful towards the Lord?

_____

_____

_____

_____

_____

_____

_____

_____

Worship demands a sacrifice—it has to cost something. How has God led you in acts of worship lately? What things have you handed over to Him in worship?

_____

_____

_____

_____

_____

_____

_____

_____

_____

_____

When's the last time you found yourself truly humbled and grateful at the feet of Jesus? How did that worship alter your relationship and intimacy with Him?

_____

_____

_____

_____

_____

_____

_____

_____

_____

_____

> *Let us consider how to stir one another to love and good works, not neglecting to meet together as is the habit of some . . . encourage each other all the more as you see the Day is drawing near.*
>
> —*Hebrews 10:24-25 (ESV)*

Consider the scripture above and answer the following questions:

What are some of the factors in our present day that keep people from meeting together regularly in a local church?

_____

_____

_____

_____

_____

_____

How can we stay faithful to meeting even in our current circumstances and with the challenges you identified above?

_____

_____

_____

_____

_____

_____

_____

_____

Why is it important that "the Day is drawing near"? How does this make our mission as the local church and our meeting together even more urgent?

_____

_____

_____

_____

_____

_____

_____

_____

_____

_____

_____

WE > ME

"Jesus is building His church, and He wants every one of His children to be a part of a local life-giving church. He wants us in community."

As you read
Chapter 5:
"We > Me"
in *Flourish*,
review, reflect
on, and respond
to the text by
answering
the following
questions.

REVIEW, REFLECT, AND RESPOND:

How does it make you feel to know that
God chose you personally to be part of His
family? Does this change your perspective
on the local church and its purpose?

_____

_____

_____

_____

_____

_____

_____

Why do you think so many believers think
that they can love God but not love His
people? How does this mindset limit the
richness of these believers' experience as
part of the body of Christ?

_____

_____

_____

_____

_____

_____

_____

_____

_____

_____

_____

> *"For God so loved the world that he gave his only son that whoever believes in him wouldn't perish, but have everlasting life."*
>
> *—John 3:16 (NIV)*

Consider the scripture above and answer the following questions:

How is the reconciliation that Jesus brings both vertical and horizontal?

_____

_____

_____

_____

_____

Why do you think Satan tries to convince us that this reconciliation is only vertical (that there's little or no reconciliation to be had with others)?

_____

_____

_____

_____

Based on this chapter, how do all of Christ's biggest commandments intrinsically involve people and relationships?

_____

_____

_____

_____

_____

_____

_____

In general, do you find yourself pursuing horizontal reconciliation and community in this season of your life? Why do you think this is?

_____

_____

_____

_____

_____

How might God want to multiply your joy, your influence, and your calling by connecting you with other believers?

_____

_____

_____

_____

_____

_____

What's one concrete step you can take this week to begin meeting together with other believers, stirring one another up to love and good works?

_____

_____

_____

_____

_____

RIGHT ALIGNMENTS FOR RIGHT ASSIGNMENTS

"If we want to be fruitful and multiply, we have to be willing to die to our self-will and selfishness to have meaningful, purpose-driven relationships in the kingdom of God."

As you read
Chapter 6:
"Right
Alignments
for Right
Assignments"
in *Flourish*,
review, reflect
on, and respond
to the text by
answering
the following
questions.

REVIEW, REFLECT, AND RESPOND:

What unexpected or unvoiced expectations
have you placed on the relationships in your
life? What expectations have they placed on
you? How do these expectations affect the
quality of our connections with one another?

_____

_____

_____

_____

_____

_____

_____

_____

_____

_____

_____

_____

Which hurts have you experienced in the
church that make it difficult for you to want
to move towards other believers or take part
in corporate worship?

_____

_____

_____

_____

_____

_____

What difficult conversations do you need to initiate with others that may begin to heal some of that hurt? (Keep in mind that, in certain situations, this may not be your responsibility, or it may not be safe to engage with people who have no intention of changing their behavior.)

_____

_____

_____

_____

_____

_____

_____

Are there any areas in which God is calling you to extend forgiveness towards others, whether or not reconciliation with them is possible at this time?

_____

_____

_____

_____

_____

Have you ever served under an unhealthy leader, like David did under Saul? What complications and difficulties do this scenario present?

_____

_____

_____

_____

_____

According to this chapter, what are some practical steps we can take to serve well under our current leadership, even if they're not perfect?

_____

_____

_____

_____

_____

_____

What might be a warning sign that it's time to "flee," as David did, from extremely abusive leadership? How can we still be honoring even as we leave?

_____

_____

_____

_____

_____

_____

> *"'The LORD has told me to go to Bethel.'*
>
> *But Elisha replied, 'As surely as the LORD lives and you yourself live, I will never leave you!'*
>
> *So they went down together to Bethel."*
>
> *—2 Kings 2:2 (NLT)*

Consider the scripture above and answer the following questions:

How do the stories of Elijah and Ruth and the author's personal stories illustrate the importance of being under spiritual authority?

_____

_____

_____

_____

_____

_____

_____

In your own words, what power does humbling ourselves under spiritual authority give us? How does it open us up to the power and purposes of God?

_____

_____

_____

_____

_____

_____

_____

SPARKS WILL FLY

"Challenges and conflicts are inevitable, whether they be in marriage, family, friendships, businesses, or churches."

As you read Chapter 7: "Sparks Will Fly" in *Flourish*, review, reflect on, and respond to the text by answering the following questions.

REVIEW, REFLECT, AND RESPOND:

How can conflict actually sharpen and improve us as a body?

_____

_____

_____

_____

_____

_____

Think of a time that conflict made you better as a person and taught you important lessons. What did you learn from this "friction" with others?

_____

_____

_____

_____

_____

_____

Given the nature of imperfect people and inevitable conflict this side of heaven, why is humility essential to our relationships?

_____

_____

_____

_____

_____

_____

How can conflict be a door to deeper intimacy? When have you seen this exemplified in your own relationships?

_____

_____

_____

_____

_____

Are there any relationships in your life in which you recognize a need for forgiveness on your part towards someone else? What makes it difficult to forgive this person/these people?

_____

_____

_____

_____

_____

Take some time to pray and record your thoughts after finishing this chapter. Ask God to help you move towards other believers in a healthy way, with wisdom and grace, humbly and with the same forgiveness He's offered you. Ask for His help in discerning which relationships are key to His purposes for your life, so that you can both be edified by these individuals and edify them as well!

_____

_____

_____

_____

_____

_____

> *"Father, forgive us of our [transgressions] as we forgive those who [transgress] against us."*
>
> *—Matthew 6:12 (author paraphrase)*

Consider the scripture above and answer the following questions:

What are some of the tenants of Biblical conflict resolution found in this chapter that especially resonate with you?

_____

_____

_____

_____

_____

_____

_____

_____

Why is it necessary to recognize the forgiveness we've received from God in order to turn around and give it to others?

_____

_____

_____

_____

_____

_____

_____

_____

_____

THE REAL "F" WORD

*"Each and every one of us can be wrong
and still think we're right."*

REVIEW, REFLECT, AND RESPOND:

Why is offense so powerful? How does it keep us from leaning fully into relationships and fellowshipping with God's church?

_____

_____

_____

_____

_____

_____

_____

_____

_____

_____

What's the danger in believing we're always right?

_____

_____

_____

_____

_____

_____

_____

_____

_____

_____

_____

> *"Why do you see the speck that is in your brother's eye, but do not notice the log that is in your own eye? How can you say to your brother, 'Brother, let me take out the speck that is in your eye,' when you yourself do not see the log that is in your own eye? You hypocrite, first take the log out of your own eye, and then you will see clearly to take out the speck that is in your brother's eye."*
>
> —Luke 6:41-42 (ESV)

Consider the scripture above and answer the following questions:

What "logs" do you need to remove from your own eye? What is the Holy Spirit convicting you about—the unforgiveness and offenses that are keeping you from seeing clearly?

_____

_____

_____

_____

_____

How do we pull down the "fences" or established ways we think about others? How might you need God's help in redefining your perspective of others?

_____

_____

_____

_____

_____

_____

How does offense cause our love to "grow cold" towards others—
and potentially even towards God?

_____

_____

_____

_____

_____

_____

_____

_____

Pain is real. But God always brings purpose out of that pain.
Knowing and trusting Him, ask for His help in forgiving others—
in letting go of offense. Spend some time in prayer asking for His
guidance.

SHIFT HAPPENS

"A shift in God's favor can happen. But if we get negative, we get out of position."

As you read Chapter 9: "Shift Happens" in *Flourish*, review, reflect on, and respond to the text by answering the following questions.

REVIEW, REFLECT, AND RESPOND:

Looking at the different biblical stories in this chapter, which ones stand out to you? Which individuals had the opportunity to become bitter and negative but chose to stay where God had placed them and trust in Him?

_____

_____

_____

_____

_____

_____

_____

_____

Why is it essential to see ourselves as God sees us? What happens, conversely, when we lose sight of our identity in Christ and begin to view things from an earthly perspective?

_____

_____

_____

_____

_____

_____

_____

_____

What are some practical ways that you can begin to come under spiritual authority right now?

_____

_____

_____

_____

_____

_____

_____

_____

Why might this humbling and submission process be difficult?

_____

_____

_____

_____

_____

_____

How did Jesus model this principle during His earthly life? How does His legacy encourage and exhort you to do the same?

_____

_____

_____

_____

_____

_____

> *"Humble yourselves, therefore, under God's mighty hand that He may lift you up in due time."*
>
> —*1 Peter 5:6 (NIV)*

Consider the scripture above and answer the following questions:

How does it free us up that we don't need to promote or champion ourselves? How does it make you feel to know that God is already working out His purposes in your life?

_____

_____

_____

_____

_____

_____

_____

How does the story of Ephraim and Manasseh illustrate this principle?

_____

_____

_____

_____

_____

_____

_____

_____

_____

INTIMACY AND IMPACT

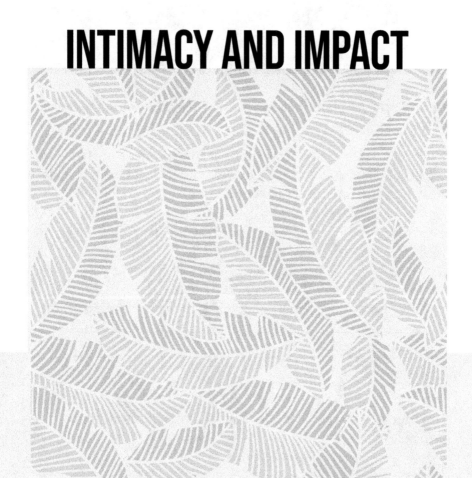

*"If you want to flourish in life, it matters whom
you choose to align with for God's glory."*

As you read Chapter 10: "Intimacy and Impact" in *Flourish*, review, reflect on, and respond to the text by answering the following questions.

REVIEW, REFLECT, AND RESPOND:

What insights and truths do you glean from the story of the sons of Korah?

_____

_____

_____

_____

_____

_____

_____

_____

_____

Is your background one of being closely aligned with the people of God or far from them? How does this impact your current journey of becoming closer with God's people?

_____

_____

_____

_____

_____

_____

_____

_____

_____

> *"For God knew His people in advance. And He chose them to become like His Son so that His Son would be the firstborn among many brothers and sisters."*
>
> —*Romans 8:29 (NLT)*

Consider the scripture above and answer the following questions:

How does it change your perspective of the church to think of yourself as one of many brothers and sisters, with Christ being the firstborn?

_____

_____

_____

_____

_____

Why is it essential that we stay plugged into Christ, abiding in Him, in order to be fruitful and multiply?

_____

_____

_____

_____

What role do God's people, our spiritual siblings, play in our fruitfulness?

_____

_____

_____

_____

Do you currently have any accountability partners or people whom you fully trust? If not, what might be holding you back from seeking out these relationships?

_____

_____

_____

_____

In your own words, explain the difference between intimacy and impact (family and function), as described in this chapter. Why is this distinction important, especially in a worldly culture that's very works-based?

_____

_____

_____

_____

What next steps do you need to take to be more firmly planted in God's house and intimately connected with its people?

_____

_____

_____

_____

WE WILL ROCK YOU

"When we go through challenges and struggles, they're not meant to take us out. They're meant to cause us to be unique and to step into our greatness."

As you read Chapter 11: "We Will Rock You" in *Flourish*, review, reflect on, and respond to the text by answering the following questions.

REVIEW, REFLECT, AND RESPOND:

What challenges and struggles have caused you to step more fully into your purpose?

_____

_____

_____

_____

_____

_____

Are there any challenges in your present life that are serving this purpose? Identify how they're shaping you or how it is difficult to do that in the midst of the struggle.

_____

_____

_____

_____

_____

_____

_____

How does it encourage you that none of the people God used in the Bible were perfect—they were only available?

_____

_____

_____

_____

_____

What generational chains might you be called to break in your family and/or community?

_____

_____

_____

_____

_____

Do you tend to look in front of you or behind you? Why do you think this is? How can you begin to shift your gaze forward?

_____

_____

_____

_____

_____

_____

_____

_____

What practical next steps or final thoughts do you have as we draw nearer to the conclusion of this study? Take some time to pray through what God has taught you so far.

_____

_____

_____

_____

> *"Your servant has struck down both lions and bears, and this uncircumcised Philistine shall be like one of them, for he has defied the armies of the living God."*
>
> —*1 Samuel 17:36 (ESV)*

Consider the scripture above and answer the following questions:

How did David's previous responsibilities prepare him for facing Goliath?

_____

_____

_____

_____

Why is it important that David's focus was on God's glory and not his own?

_____

_____

_____

_____

What preparation has God provided for you that will help you step more fully into what He has next for you?

_____

_____

_____

_____

_____

SUCCESS STARTS ON SUNDAY

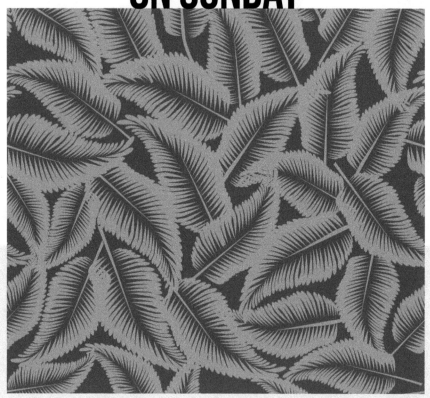

"We can't do it all and have it all. We have the power to choose how we invest our time and our lives."

As you read Chapter 12: "Success Starts on the Sunday" in *Flourish*, review, reflect on, and respond to the text by answering the following questions.

REVIEW, REFLECT, AND RESPOND:

Do you tend to spend time off being productive and checking things off your to-do list? What's the difference?

_____

_____

_____

_____

_____

_____

_____

_____

_____

_____

Why is *Sabbath* essential to our health and our calling?

_____

_____

_____

_____

_____

_____

_____

_____

_____

_____

_____

_____

> *"You have six days each week for your ordinary work, but the seventh day is a Sabbath day of rest dedicated to the LORD your God."*
>
> —*Exodus 20:9-10 (NLT)*

Consider the scripture above and answer the following questions:

How do stopping and resting demonstrate faith in God?

_____

_____

_____

_____

_____

What other benefits come with taking a day, or a set period of time, to cease work and activity?

_____

_____

_____

_____

_____

How does "Sabbathing" help us refocus on our purpose in the midst of a chaotic world?

_____

_____

_____

_____

What final thoughts do you have as you finish this study? In what ways has God provided enlightenment, encouragement, and conviction?

_____

_____

_____

_____

_____

_____

_____

What are your next steps? Who do you need to connect or reconnect with? Spend some time in prayer asking for His guidance and strength to move forward into your purpose with the people of God!

_____

_____

_____

_____

_____